CONVERSATIONS
WITH A
DYING MAN

CONVERSATIONS WITH A DYING MAN

BY

SAMUEL RUTHERFORD

REFORMATION PRESS

2017

British Library Cataloguing in Publication Data

ISBN 978-1-912042-00-5

© Reformation Press 2017

Originally published in 1649 as
The Last and Heavenly Speeches,
and Glorious Departure,
of John Gordon, Viscount Kenmure

Published by Reformation Press
11 Churchill Drive, Stornoway
Isle of Lewis, Scotland HS1 2NP

www.reformationpress.co.uk

Also available as a Kindle e-book
ISBN 978-1-912042-01-2

Printed by www.lulu.com

Contents

৪০৫৪

Foreword

THIS book was first published anonymously in 1649. From strong internal and external evidence, it has always been accepted that the author was Samuel Rutherford (*c.* 1660–1661). The original title was *The Last and Heavenly Speeches, and Glorious Departure, of John Gordon, Viscount Kenmure.* This new Reformation Press edition has been retitled *Conversations with a Dying Man.*

Rutherford records the dying days of John Gordon, Viscount Kenmure, a presbyterian nobleman who had been instrumental in settling Rutherford in the parish of Anwoth. Kenmure had made a bold profession of faith but in 1633 he had failed to support God's cause in the Scottish Parliament. This caused grief not only to Kenmure but also to the other Scottish presbyterian noblemen. The following year he became seriously ill and it soon became evident that he would not recover. He was sorely tried on account of his unworthy behaviour and Rutherford dealt faithfully and lovingly with him. The book relates the seven conversations Rutherford had with Kenmure, together with Kenmure's reconciliation with his adversaries and the advice he gave to friends as he neared eternity.

The book also includes biographies of Viscount Kenmure and his wife, who is well known as one of Rutherford's correspondents. These sketches of their lives have been adapted from an *Introductory Memoir* provided by Thomas Murray (1792–1872) for an edition of the book printed in 1828. The historical and biographical information has been expanded where necessary in order to provide extra background details, and factual errors have been corrected. Footnotes from the 1828 edition are marked as such, to distinguish them from extra footnotes provided for the present edition.

Readers who wish to learn more about Rutherford's views of Viscount Kenmure will be interested to know that three manuscript Latin poems relating to him have recently been discovered in the National Library of Scotland. It is believed that Samuel Rutherford was the author of the poems, which comprise a short epitaph, a confession of sin, and an address to Scottish Protestant nobles. The latter two poems are written from the viewpoint of the dying Viscount Kenmure. The three poems have been translated into English and published online in 2017 (www.philological.bham.ac.uk/rutherford).

Rutherford had his own characteristic style of writing. Some words were exclusively Scottish and certain English words have either altered their meanings with the passage of time or have become obsolete. In order to preserve the original character of Rutherford's writing, such words have been left unaltered in the text and modern equivalents given either in brackets or in footnotes. The text has been repunctuated to conform to current conventions and the layout has been arranged in order to make the book attractive to the twenty-first century reader—these changes have been accomplished with the minimum interference to Rutherford's text.

It is a solemn matter for any person to approach death. This was especially the case for Viscount Kenmure when his conscience testified to his unfaithful behaviour and his desertion of the cause of God in pursuit of worldly preferment. It is instructive to read how Rutherford faithfully and tenderly dealt with his long-standing friend, without fear or favour. The pastor of Anwoth brought the erring nobleman to repentance for his deeds. At the end, Kenmure died with a well-founded hope of salvation—he passed from time to eternity 'sweetly and holily, and his end was peace'.

In issuing *Conversations with a Dying Man* it is the prayer of the Publisher that the thought-provoking book will be profitable to many readers.

THE PUBLISHER
Stornoway
June 2017

ഇൽ

Biographical notes

John Gordon, Viscount Kenmure

JOHN GORDON was born in 1599, the eldest son of Sir Robert Gordon of Lochinvar (c. 1565–1628) and Lady Isabel Ruthven[1] (1577–1616), daughter of the 1st Earl of Gowrie. The Gordon family had been landowners in Galloway for more than three centuries and they adopted Reformation principles at an early stage in the sixteenth century.

It appears that John Gordon did not have the advantage of a religious upbringing. Though Sir Robert Gordon was not a pious man and the household lacked vital religion, nevertheless the young John went on to spend time in the household of the godly presbyterian minister, John Welsh[2] of Ayr (1568–1622), when Welsh was in exile at St-Jean-d'Angély in France. John Gordon benefited from the company of the banished minister and the practical piety in his household. There was a discerni-

---

[1] The name is pronounced 'Rivven' in Scotland.
[2] Also spelled Welch. He was born in Dumfriesshire and was educated at the University of Edinburgh. He became a minister in Selkirk and later in Kirkcudbright and then in Ayr. His preaching offended King James VI of Scotland and led to his imprisonment and then banishment to France. There he rapidly became fluent in French and continued his labours as a minister in the Huguenot Church in three locations, the last of which was St-Jean-d'Angély in southwest France. Welsh returned to London when his health declined, and died there in 1622. His wife, Elizabeth, was a daughter of John Knox. His grandson was John Welsh (c. 1624–1681), minister of Irongray in Dumfriesshire, a leader of the Covenanters.

ble change in John Gordon's personal behaviour when he returned from France to the family residence at Rusco Castle in the parish of Anwoth.

John Gordon now sought to communicate the blessings of a gospel ministry to those around him. At that time two other parishes were linked to Anwoth, with the result that public worship took place there only on alternate Sabbaths. The parishioners of Anwoth wrote of these circumstances many years later: 'Our souls were under that miserable extreme famine of the Word, that we had only the poor help of one sermon every second Sabbath, by reason of a most inconvenient union with two other kirks [churches].' After much delay and difficulty, John Gordon succeeded in getting Anwoth disjoined from the other two parishes, so that it was able to call its own minister.

John Livingstone was the first man invited to become pastor of Anwoth but instead he accepted a request to assist the minister of Torphichen in the Presbytery of Linlithgow. Livingstone later wrote in his autobiography: 'The Lord provided a great deal better for the people of Anwoth, for they got that worthy servant of Christ, Mr Samuel Rutherford, whose praise is in all the reformed churches.' Rutherford was settled in Anwoth in 1627.

John Gordon married Lady Jane Campbell some time before Rutherford came to Anwoth. By their influence and example, the Gordons cooperated with their new minister in promoting a spirit of true religion among the parishioners. However, less than two years after Rutherford's induction the couple moved to Edinburgh, and Rutherford viewed this as one of the severest trials he met with after he had entered on the ministry.

Rutherford corresponded with them by letters on religious subjects. He assured them that his constant prayer was that God would bless them by his Spirit and increasingly cultivate and confirm their Christian graces and dispositions.

John Gordon and his wife returned from Edinburgh and settled at Kenmure Castle, some twenty miles from Anwoth. At some point he had been knighted and was now known as Sir John Gordon of Lochinvar. He was a strong supporter of the Stuart monarchy. At his Scottish coronation in Edinburgh on 8th May 1633, Charles I elevated him to the peerage, bestowing on him the titles Viscount of Kenmure and Lord Lochinvar. Rutherford wrote to Lady Kenmure, 'I bless our Lord Jesus Christ, who hath brought you home again to your country, from that place where you have seen with your eyes that which our Lord's truth taught you before, to wit, that worldly glory is nothing but a vapour, a shadow, the foam of the water, or something less and lighter, even nothing; and that our Lord hath not without cause said in his word, "The countenance or fashion of this world passeth away."'

These observations on the part of Rutherford were probably occasioned by the worldly-minded and ambitious views which her husband had recently displayed. John Gordon had become comparatively indifferent both as to his own progress in holiness and to the public interests of religion. He cherished the hope of still higher dignity than knighthood: he coveted the title of Earl of Gowrie. The background to this requires a short digression into the history of his mother's family and its role in Scottish political intrigues.

Gordon's mother was one of ten daughters of William Ruthven, the 1st Earl of Gowrie. In 1582, several Presbyterian nobles, led by the Earl of Gowrie, abducted the fifteen-year-old King James VI of Scotland during a visit to Ruthven Castle near Perth, an event known to historians as the Ruthven Raid. The nobles intended to reform the government of Scotland, to limit the influence of French and pro-Catholic policy, and to prevent or manage the return of Mary, Queen of Scots, from England.

The conspirators kept the king captive at various locations for ten months but he gained his freedom at St Andrews in July 1583. The Earl of Gowrie was pardoned for his role in this affair, but due to continued plotting against the king he was beheaded for high treason in May 1584. All Gowrie's honours were forfeited and his lands were divided among the king's favourites in a process known as attainder.

Two years later in 1586, the attainder was reversed and William Ruthven's eldest son James, the 2nd Earl, was restored as Earl of Gowrie and Lord Ruthven. James Ruthven died later that year and a younger brother, John, became the 3rd Earl in childhood. These earls were brothers of Kenmure's mother, Isabel Ruthven.

John Ruthven, the 3rd Earl of Ruthven, allegedly continued the family intrigues against King James and was killed during a visit of the king to Gowrie House in Perth in 1600, concluding an event known as the Gowrie Conspiracy. Later that year the Scottish Parliament decreed that the estates of the Ruthvens should be forfeited and their family name and honours were abolished.

With this background to the events leading to the extinction of the House of Gowrie, we return to the history of John Gordon. After the death of King James, Gordon sought to gain the favour of King Charles I, so that the title of Earl of Gowrie would be revived and bestowed on him. He is said to have sold a family estate in the Scottish Borders to provide a substantial bribe to the Duke of Buckingham to promote Kenmure's views about the earldom. This ploy was unsuccessful as the Duke died the following day.

Kenmure professed to retain his theological and ecclesiastical principles. However, his worldly aspirations led him to forsake the path of duty when King Charles wished to subvert the presbyterian principles of the Church of Scotland. When the Scottish Parliament discussed Charles' proposals, Kenmure claimed to be unwell in order to avoid opposing the king. He left Edinburgh and went to Kenmure Castle. Afterwards this step filled him with the most bitter sorrow and he said, 'I deserted the Parliament for fear of incurring the indignation of my prince, and the loss of further honour, which I certainly expected.'

When Kenmure left Edinburgh, he took with him Mr George Gillespie as his domestic chaplain. This indicates that the sense of religion had not been entirely effaced. However, it seems that he did not avail himself as much as he ought of that excellent minister's instructions. Indeed, on his deathbed, Kenmure expressed regret for this to Gillespie in these words: 'I would I had paid better heed to many of your words. I might have gotten good by the means God gave me; but I made no use of them.'

After the ignominious return to Kenmure Castle, Gordon remained there during the following year, venturing only once to pay a brief visit to Edinburgh. At the end of August 1634, little more than a year after withdrawing from Parliament, he developed a fever, which led rapidly to his premature death at the age of thirty-five.

Viscount Kenmure came to see his previous cowardly conduct in its true character when he contrasted his own behaviour to that of the most eminent both of the clergy and laity, who continued to make the most strenuous exertions to expose the nature of Charles' intentions and to obviate their effects on the church. 'God knoweth that I deserted the last Parliament with the fearful wrestlings of my conscience, my light paying me home within, when I seemed to be glad and joyful before men.' On his deathbed in particular, he was the victim of the most poignant sorrow and remorse. The voice of conscience smote him with an irresistible force and he would willingly have sacrificed all his interests and honours in this life if he could have cancelled or reversed the dereliction of duty and the other offences of which he had been guilty. He confessed, 'I have found the weight of the Lord's hand upon me for not giving testimony for the Lord my God, when I had occasion once in my life at the last parliament. For this foul fault, how fierce have I felt the wrath of the Lord my God! My soul hath raged and roared: I have been ripped up [grieved] to the heart. ... Would to God I had such an occasion again to testify my love to the Lord! For all the earth should I not do as I have done, tell them. ... Woe, woe be to honours or anything else bought with the loss of peace of conscience and God's favour!'

However, God did not leave him in despair. Samuel Rutherford had been in Irvine, probably visiting the renowned minister, David Dickson.[3] On his return journey to Anwoth, he

---

[3] David Dickson (c. 1583–1663) was ordained as minister of Irvine in 1618. His ministry there was singularly blessed by God. In 1650 he

called at Kenmure Castle and found his friend rapidly deteriorating. Viscount Kenmure rejoiced at the arrival of a minister whom he so greatly esteemed. He begged Rutherford to remain and was glad that he agreed. Rutherford remained with Kenmure until his death, which took place about two weeks later on 12th September 1634.

Rutherford details in this book the conversations he had with Kenmure. The viscount was well aware that he was dying and the realisation made him afraid. 'I never dreamt', said he, 'that death had such a terrible, austere, and gloomy countenance. ... I dare not die; howbeit, I know I must die.' Rutherford proceeded with great earnestness and judgment to show him the principles and views which the Gospel teaches and to point out the reasons for his fear of death. Above all, he constantly presented to Kenmure's view 'the blood of sprinkling' as the only effectual balm for his wounded spirit and as the only 'anchor of his hope, sure and stedfast'. And, notwithstanding some doubts and fears on the part of Kenmure, and the interference of a clergyman of less sound views, Rutherford succeeded, through divine grace, in accomplishing such a reformation in the sentiments and hopes of this nobleman, that his death has always been regarded as conspicuously that of a righteous man.

A few minutes before his departure, Rutherford asked Kenmure if he should pray. Kenmure was unable to speak and turned his eye to the pastor. The minister engaged in prayer

---

was appointed to the divinity chair in the University of Edinburgh but was ejected from the chair for declining to take the oath of supremacy at the Restoration of Charles II. Dickson was the author of several well-known and influential works.

accordingly, and during that last prayer Viscount Kenmure was observed 'joyfully smiling, and looking up with glorious look'. His breathing and pulse stopped at the exact moment Rutherford concluded his prayer with 'Amen'.

Such were the life and death of this nobleman. Little is told of his life as little is known. However, the circumstances connected with his dying days are minutely recorded in the following treatise.[4] It is an extremely valuable and instructive work, containing a simple but forcible delineation of the upbraidings and anguish of a wounded conscience, and the hope, consolation and joy which, through the mediation of a Saviour, the Gospel is designed and calculated to afford.

ℰℭ

Lady Kenmure

Lady Jane Kenmure, whose name must be known to every individual acquainted with the religious history of the seventeenth century, came from a prominent Covenanting family. She was a daughter of Archibald, 7th Earl of Argyll and her brother, also named Archibald (1st Marquess of Argyll), was beheaded in 1661 for his adherence to Presbyterian principles and to the Solemn League and Covenant of 1643.

---

[4] In addition to the following treatise, Rutherford composed a long elegiac poem on Kenmure's death, *In Joannem Gordonum Kenmarii Vicecomitem Apotheosis*. Rutherford also dedicated his first publication (*Exercitationes Apologeticæ pro Divina Gratia* [*Apologetical Exercises in favour of Divine Grace*], Amsterdam, 1636) to Viscount Kenmure and *The Trial and Triumph of Faith* (London, 1645), to Lady Kenmure.

Viscount Kenmure on his deathbed gave an honourable and ample testimony of his wife's holiness and goodness, and of the respectful kindness she had shown to him. He earnestly craved her forgiveness where he had offended her, and desired her to make the Lord her comfort. Before his death 'the Lord had taken away from her many children'. She was left a widow with a single surviving son; the boy had never been very healthy and died in 1639, five years after the death of his father.

Lady Kenmure subsequently remarried in 1640. Her second husband, the Honourable Henry Montgomery, was the second son to the Earl of Eglinton, 'an active and faithful friend of Christ's Kirk'. His religious views were identical to hers. Sadly, he died soon after their marriage, which was childless.

Under all these bereaving dispensations she seems to have been eminently supported by the consoling influences of religious truth, and not to have sorrowed as those that have no hope—a state of mind which Rutherford's letters to her on these mournful occurrences were admirably calculated to produce or confirm. This celebrated divine wrote, 'Though I must, out of some experience, say that the mourning for the husband of your youth is, by God's own word, the heaviest worldly sorrow, and this be the weightiest burden that ever lay on your back, yet you know, if ye shall wait on the Lord, who hideth his face for a while, that it lieth on his honour and truth, to be a husband to the widow.' After the death of a daughter, he observed: 'You have lost a child. Nay, *she* is not lost to *you*, who is found to Christ; she is not sent away, but only sent before. Like unto a star which, going out of our sight, does not die and vanish, but shineth in another hemisphere, so ye see her not, yet she doth shine in another country.' In another letter he said, 'The temporal loss of creatures dear to you here may be the more easily endured, when the gain of One, who only hath immortality, groweth.'

Lady Kenmure did not enjoy good health or a strong constitution. Rutherford, in his correspondence with her, occasionally alluded to the weakly condition of her body. Yet she attained to great old age. She was alive in 1672 but her subsequent history and death are not recorded.

During her whole life, Lady Kenmure maintained an intimate friendship and connection with the most eminent Christians. In addition to many others, she kept up a close correspondence with Samuel Rutherford. His numerous letters to her (which do equal honour to both parties) breathe a spirit of the purest and most elevated piety. She was distinguished for goodness as well as for charity and generosity. Her charity was in a special manner extended to those who were in poverty or exile for conscience sake.

Rutherford's words are apposite: 'It is not the antiquity of your families, nor the long descent of an ancient pedigree through many noble and princely branches, that can make you noble. True nobility consists in that adoption by which you are made the sons of God, children of the King of kings, and brethren of the eternal Son of God. The titles of this nobility are not written in old, rotten, or moulded parchments, but are more ancient than the heavens. … Fools may be lifted up, and think what they please of civil nobility; but the most royal blood is the most religious heart.'

ഔൟ

19

Samuel Rutherford's dedication

For the whole Nobility of Scotland, and others having voice in Parliament or Committees

WHEREAS the testimony of a dying nobleman, deeply wounded in spirit, is the surest and most unsuspected argument of the truth, I have thought fit to make known to all the lovers of God and the work of his right hand, the heavy pangs of conscience and torment of mind, wherewith a nobleman, not long since, was exercised upon his deathbed for not countenancing the cause of God when he was publicly called thereunto in Parliament; and to discover [reveal] the fountain of those terrors and griefs, that others may learn, by his example, not to displease our dreadful [awe-inspiring] Lord Jesus Christ either by unsound dealing or withdrawing themselves from his work. And seeing it was that late nobleman's earnest desire that all should be discovered and laid open to you, Right Honourable, it shall not be impertinent [irrelevant] (especially in this condition of time) to acquaint you with this following relation [account].

John, late Viscount Kenmure, having come to the Parliament held at Edinburgh June 1633, was present the first day, did stay but some few days thereafter, not having courage to glorify God by his presence when his cause was in hand, deserted the Parliament under pretence that his body was sick, [and] went home to his own dwelling house of Kenmure in Galloway. And as Jonas or David, [he] slept securely in his sin about the space of one year, without any check of conscience. About the beginning of August 1634, his affairs occasioned his return to Edinburgh, where he remained some few days, not knowing that with the ending of his affairs he was to end his life.

He returned home with some alteration of bodily health, and from day to day sickened, till the 12th of September next ensuing, which was to him fatal, and the day of his death. But the Lord had other thought than that this nobleman should slip out of the world unobserved, and therefore would not have him to die without some sense of his sin. Therefore it pleased the Lord to afflict his body with sickness, to shake his soul with fears, to drop in bitterness in his spirit, and make him altogether sensible [aware] of the power of eternal wrath for his own good and the good of others in after ages, who may be warned by his example, never to be wanting [lacking] to the cause of God when they have any opportunity, and never to wrong their conscience, which is a tender piece, and must not be touched.

So, as Nahaz, king of the Ammonites, would make no accommodation with the inhabitants of Jabesh-Gilead (1 Samuel 11) but upon that condition that first he should thrust out the right eye to every one of them, so Satan makes himself never master of men till first he thrusts out the right eye of their understanding. Hence is it that the false hopes of carnal men blind and deceive their minds, many times to their eternal destruction, making them to see things in false glasses [mirrors], showing them either the profit, pleasures or preferment, with the fair flourishes of foolish expectations or deluding promises. But under this bait Satan hides the sting and torment of conscience, not suffering them to see how

21

bitter a thing it is to be any ways wanting to a glorious and dreadful Lord for any by-respect [personal ends]. This is the way how Satan has ensnared many mighty, wise and noble men, making them to nibble at the golden bait, and worship that gold in the coin that they would have abhorred in a molten image, and so catching the wise in their craftiness. And as the Apostle speaks (2 Timothy 3:13), when they are deceiving, they consider not that they are deceived themselves, and are so blinded that they become confident of the constancy of sublunary [earthly] things, not so much as thinking how unstable is the foundation of that house, honour or preferment that is laid upon the ruins of God's house, wanting [lacking] illumination to see or hope anything beyond time or death, which is so strict a porter [doorkeeper], that it will not suffer any to come in or go out of this world, but stripped and naked.

But now, Right Honourable, when I am to represent to you how fearfully the spirit of this nobleman was wounded (whereof the writer hereof was an eye-witness), I shall not think that any will so construct it as to have been a fit of madness or melancholy. I know that there be many mockers who will not believe that there is any such thing as the inexpressible trouble of a troubled spirit, though Job and Jeremiah, David, Hezekiah, and God's eternal Word have given very many expressions to the contrary, as these: 'Hath God forgotten to be merciful?' and Solomon (Proverbs 18:14), 'But a wounded spirit who can bear?' Some have chattered as cranes and mourned as doves; others casting out fearful cries, as owls in the desert; others screeching as the pelican; and as this nobleman said when his conscience was upon the rack, 'My soul hath raged and roared.'

I shall further desire you earnestly to consider that the trouble and tempest of this nobleman's mind was not for voicing [speaking] against, but only deserting the cause of God, which is scarcely counted a fault in these times. This may teach every man to tremble. Rather than to be any ways wanting [lacking] to the cause of God, but still to stand to it with courage for the truth, the peace of conscience being such an inesteemable [inestimable] treasure. So the wound of a wounded spirit is a most inexpressible terror; nor none can [neither can one] describe it but he who has tasted and tried the same. It impairs the health, dries up the blood, wastes away the marrow, pines away the flesh, consumes away the bones, makes pleasure painful, and shortens life: no wisdom can counsel it, no counsel can advise it, no advice can persuade it, no assuagement can cure it, no eloquence can affray it, no enchanter can charm it. Who dares meet with the wrath of these? O holy Lord of Hosts, who can put to silence the voice of desperation? It breeds such hurly-burlies in the mind of him that labours under it, that when it is day he wishes for night, and when it is night he would have day again: his meat does not nourish him; his dreams are filled with fears, his sleep forsakes him, all outward comforts are uncomfortable.

Then consider that if in this life the torments of the soul be so fearful, how much more terrible shall it be to sustain the torments of hell, where that which is here finite is there infinite; where that which is here measurable is there unmeasurable? How great is that ocean of sorrow, whereof this is but a drop? How hot is the flame of that fire, whereof this is less than a spark? What will then avail Balaam's wages, or Naboth's vineyard, or Achan's wedge of gold, or Gehazi's bribe, or the lust-broker Jonadab's credit with a king's son, or Judas' thirty pieces of silver? What will avail the rich rewards of many treacherous murderous emissaries, or the mighty promises made to many night-plotting birds, who write in obscure characters, who work wisely and plot in darkness against the holy covenant and those who are dearest to the Lord, the innocents of the earth and apple of God's own eye? What will pensions and promotions to high dignities avail them who are lifted up for betraying the cause of God, Church or State?—when not only the blood of Jesus Christ, his apostles and disciples, shall be required at their hand, but all the blood from Abel to Zechariah, from Zechariah to Jesus Christ and his disciples, from them to the last martyr that suffered under the ten cruel emperors and all the popes, from them to the poor Waldenses, from them to the holy martyrs that suffered under Queen Mary of England, and all the martyrs of the massacre of Paris,[5] and all the cruelly roasted martyrs of the Spanish Inquisition, from them to that incomparable murder of the martyrs and holy ones of Ireland. When all that blood, I say, shall be required at their hand, who is able to stand before thee, O holy Lord of hosts, when thou shalt once begin to speak a word in thy wrath, and vex wicked men in thy sore displeasure?

Remember, therefore, that conscience is placed in the soul as God's own deputy and God's notary. There is nothing passes in our life, good or evil, which conscience notes not down with an indelible character—conscience writes all men's iniquities as the sin of Judah was written (Jeremiah 17:1) with a pen of iron and with the point of a diamond. Conscience does in this our pilgrimage, as travellers upon a journey—it keeps a

---

[5] Bartholomew's Day massacre of Protestants in 1572.

daily diary of everything that occurs in the whole course of our life, and then conscience is as a thousand witnesses: it's an eye-witness and a pen-witness, bringing testimony from the authentic registers and records of the court of conscience. Blessed is the man who follows the injunctions, dictates, prohibitions and determinations of a good and right-informed conscience, and hearkens to all the incitements thereof. Oh that every man would remember how dangerous a thing it is to resist the checks of conscience, for in so doing we fight not only against our own light, but against the light of the Holy Spirit! And grow to such a sottishness and induration [hardening] in sin, that no admonition is able to forewarn us, neither can any punishment work upon us when once we have suffered ourselves to be hardened by degrees: the smallest means will provoke us, but the greatest cannot revoke us from sin and impiety.

Conscience is of the nature of the eye: the least mote, the least touch, is offensive to it, and yet the learned physicians affirm that, although of all the parts of the body it be the most tender, yet if that web which is called *schirrus oculi*[6] come once upon it, of the most tender and sensible [sensitive] member it becomes the most insensible [insensitive] of all the body. This should instruct all men to fear the Lord greatly and tremble at his Word, to be exact and strict in watchfulness, fervent and frequent in prayer, lest through long custom in sin the conscience come to a palpable induration and so, as the Apostle speaks (Ephesians 4:19), 'past all feeling'.

David (Psalm 37:37) desires that we should observe and we shall find that the upright man shall have peace at last, which

---

[6] A firm, fibrous, scarring condition of the eye.

follows the warfare of this life, and brings glory and immortality with unwithering [durable] crowns; yet there be many so foolish to get the first peace that they lose the second. Saul would have peace with men, but lost his peace with God himself and his crown. The Jews refused peace with Jesus Christ to have peace with the Romans, and when they had killed Jesus Christ, they lost their peace both with God and the Romans. Look back to former times, and it shall appear that it never went well with them who, to please men, offended God, or for the faults of men would discord [disagree] with God. This way of impiety never had—nor shall have—good success, so that there is no delight to [comparable to] the delight of a good conscience: let that bird in the breast be always kept singing.

The many manifest testimonies (besides this dying Lord) that other dying persons, both in this kingdom and England, have given to this present cause, the Covenant and work of Reformation, are not to be passed in silence; for both the servants of God in the ministry, as Mr Alexander Henderson and Mr George Gillespie and many others of younger years have to the death encouraged all they left behind them to be constant therein, and have expressed their hope and confidence the Lord should yet build a glorious house for himself in this island, not to speak of the printed testimonies of the man of God and martyr, Mr George Wishart, and that heavenly man in our times, Mr John Welch. And then those who have opposed the cause, or have been misled by evil counsel, as the Lord Boyd, who was shaken with terrors (as this nobleman), and others, have expressed much terror of conscience and their deep sorrow in counterworking [opposing] the work of the right arm of the Lord—many such have been both in Scotland

and England. All this I lay before your eyes, Right Honourable, that as you would be blessed with the blessing of the right hand, and likewise have your houses built upon earth, you would exalt the holy Covenant, which, notwithstanding of all the wisdom, understanding or counsel that is against it, yet shall it be as oil among the liquors [liquids], have no intelligence [communication] with them that forsake it. Be not against it in your hearts; and, as it is said (Daniel 11:30), have no indignation against the holy Covenant.

It was the last and most earnest desire of this nobleman, Right Honourable, that being warned by his example, you might not split upon that rock nor stumble upon that stone whereupon he had stumbled when he was very weak. These were his words: 'Tell them, as they are now, so I have been, and, ere it be long, they will all follow me.' Remember, therefore, that God has set you (noblemen) as stars in the firmament of honour; upon your influence depends the whole course of the inferior world.

The offence of great ones keeps off [repels] many: the piety of great ones brings in many. It should make your hearts to tremble when it is said that few are saved: but when salvation is straitened in a more narrow compass and God's Word (1 Corinthians 1:26) hath said of noblemen that few are saved, this should stir up all men, but principally noblemen, to tremble at God's Word, and endeavour with heart and mind and might to make their calling and their election sure (2 Peter 1:10). There is nothing so base under the sun's circuit as to see those who are lifted up through civil nobility to be under the power of their lusts. John Chrysostom compares such men to a king taken prisoner, who is forced to serve with his crown

27

upon his head and his royal apparel upon him.[7] Let, therefore, spiritual nobility be superadded to civil; and then to your coronets you shall add a crown of life, and a crown of glory to your costly garments. Vicious [immoral] great men are as Uzziah, they carry their leprosy upon their brow: the faults of great men are like eclipses of the sun, most eminent [conspicuous] to all the world.

It's not the antiquity of your families, nor the long descent of an ancient pedigree through many noble or princely branches, that can make you noble. True nobility consists in that adoption by which you are made the sons of God, children of the King of kings, and brethren of the eternal Son of God. The titles of this nobility are not written in old rotten or moulded parchments, but are more ancient than the heavens. Labour, therefore, to be the sons of God by regeneration, which is the ornament of blood, and the first flower of the garland. Fools may be lifted up and think what they please of civil nobility, but the most royal blood is in the most religious heart.

If, therefore, Right Honourable, you be among men as mountains over valleys, be as those mountains of which Solomon makes mention (Canticles 4:6): be mountains of myrrh and hills of frankincense, and not as those mountains of the prophet (Hosea 4:13) which had nothing but incense and idols upon their tops and so, causing the people to err, became their snares and stumbling blocks. If you be elevated in the world as clefts [fissured cliffs] above the sea, be as watchtowers—not as misplaced beacons or louring [threatening] rocks. If you be stars, be suns to be chariots of light and life, and not prodigious

---

[7] Chrysostom (c. 349–407), Archbishop of Constantinople, was one of the most eloquent and prolific writers in the early Church.

comets to pour out malignity upon the four quarters of the world.[8] And rest assured, that how much more you are with God and united to his Majesty, so much the greater shall you be. The more conformable you are to the Lord of Glory, so much the more shall you behold the earth in contempt under your feet, and heaven in crowns over your heads.

ℰᴑ℞

---

[8] It was commonly believed that comets were bad omens.

1

Fear of approaching death —the first conversation with Rutherford

UPON the last of August 1634, which was the Sabbath of the Lord, when this nobleman's body was much weakened, he was visited with a religious and learned pastor, who then lived in Galloway, not far distant from my Lord Kenmure's house.[9] He rejoiced at the coming of this pastor to his house, and observed and spoke of a directing and all-ruling providence, who had sent to him such a man, who had been abroad [away] from Galloway for other occasions, and had returned sooner than his own expectation was, or his business could permit.

After supper about eleven hours at night my Lord drew on [began] a conference with the said pastor, saying, 'I am heavily weighted and affrighted in soul with two great burdens: the one is fear of death, the other extreme and vehement bodily pain—but the former is heavier than the latter, for I never dreamed that death had such a sour and austere, gloom, and such a terrible, and grim-like countenance. I dare not die, howbeit I know I must die. What shall I do? For I dare not

---

[9] Rutherford delicately avoids naming himself in the whole of the account.

venture in gripes [venture to struggle] with death, because I find my sins so grievous and so many, that I fear my accounts be ragged [faulty] and out of order, and not so as becometh a dying man.'

The pastor answered, 'My Lord, there is a piece of nature in all men (believers not excepted) whereby to them the first look upon death is terrible and fearful. But, my Lord, believe in him who died for you, and look the second and third time upon death's face, and if you be in Christ, you shall see Jesus hath put a white mask upon death. And I dare say if this be the time of your dissolution, I trust in God you shall both change your mind and words, for if you have a good second [assistant] in the combat (such as is only Christ), your Lord will possibly let your conscience wrestle with the fears of death. Yet he is beholding fair play, and I hope Christ Jesus shall not be a naked beholder, and say, "Deal it betwixt you," as he doth in the death of reprobates, but shall lend you help, for borrowed strength is all your strength here; yea, I hope Jesus Christ shall give death the redding [delivering] stroke. But, my Lord, I fear more the ground of your fear of death, which is (as you say) the conscience of your sins, for there can be no plea betwixt you and your Lord, if your sins be taken away in Christ, for then death loseth its action of law [legal process] against you, you being in Christ, and therefore make that sure work and fear not.'

My Lord answered, 'I have been too late in coming to God, and have deferred the time of my making my accounts so long, that I fear that I have but the foolish virgins' part of it, who came and knocked at the door of the Bridegroom too late, and so got never in.'

The pastor said, 'My Lord, I have gathered by experiences, and observed in sundry, especially in your father, that when they were plunged over head and ears in the world, and had cast down old barns and built up new again, God came in a month's space and less, and plucked them from their deceiving hopes, before they got half a bellyful—yea, or a lucky [full] mouthful—of the world. And this, my Lord, looketh like your case, for you know how deep yourself hath been in the world, in building, planting, parking [enclosing land], seeking honours, and now belike [probably] your summons are to a short day.'

My Lord answered, 'It is true, I have been busy that way, but my intentions were honest, and only to free myself of burdens and business.'

The pastor not being content with such a naked answer in such a weighty proposition, drew the conference about again to his fear of death and to a reckoning with his Lord, and said, 'My Lord, you know that it is one of the weightiest businesses that ever you put your hand to (to die) especially seeing judgment is at death's back. Faults in your life are mendable by repentance, but one wrong footstep in death is conjoined [combined] with eternal loss, for there is neither time nor place to regret of evil and bad dying. Therefore I entreat you, my Lord, by the mercies of God, by your appearance [appearing] before Christ your Judge, and by the salvation of your soul, that you would here look ere you leap, and venture not into eternity without a testificate [testimony] under Jesus Christ's hand, because it is the curse of the hypocrite (Job 20:11), "He lieth down in the grave, and his bones full of the sins of his youth."'

My Lord replied, 'When I begin to look upon my life, I think all is wrong in it, and the lateness of my reckoning affrighteth me. Therefore stay with me and show me the marks of a child of God, for you must be my second in this combat, and wait upon me.'

His Lady answered, 'My heart, you must have Jesus Christ to be your second,' unto the which he said heartily, 'Amen.'

Then said my Lord, 'But how shall I know that I am in the state of grace? For while [until] I be resolved [satisfied about it], my fears will still overburden me.'

The pastor said, 'My Lord, hardly or never doth a castaway anxiously and carefully ask the question, whether he be the child of God or not.'

Then my Lord, out of desire to be persuaded of his salvation, excepted [objected] against that mark, and said, 'I do not think that there is any reprobate in hell but he would with all his heart have the kingdom of heaven.'

The pastor having differenced [distinguished] to him what sort of desires of salvation falleth in reprobates, my Lord said, 'You never did see in me any tokens of true grace, and that is my great and only fear.'

The pastor said, 'My Lord, I was sorry to see you carried so fearfully away with temptations, and you know whether by word or writ I did give you warning that it would come to this that you see this night. I would wish your soul were deeply humbled for sin, but to your demand I say, I thought you had ever a love to the saints, and even to the poorest and sillyest [most defenceless] who carried [bore] Christ's image, howbeit they could never serve nor pleasure you in any way.

And John saith (1 John 3:14), "By this we know we are translated from death to life, because we love the brethren." With that mark he was after some objections convinced.

The pastor asked him, 'My Lord, dare you now quit your part of Christ, and subscribe an absolute resignation [relinquishment] of Jesus Christ?'

My Lord said, 'O sir, that is too hard. I hope he and I have more to do together than so. I will be advised ere I do that.'

Then my Lord asked, 'What mark is it to have judgment to discern [distinguish between] a minister called and sent of God and an hireling?' The pastor allowed it as a good mark also, and cited to him John 10:4: 'My sheep know my voice.'

ॐ

2

Conviction of sin
—the second conversation with
Rutherford

AT the second conference, the pastor urged a necessity of a deep humiliation, and said, 'My Lord, you know Christ must have such souls to work upon and not the whole.'

My Lord said, 'God knoweth, but that is a needful "must". Oh if I could get him! But sin causeth me to be jealous [distrustful] of his love, to such a man as I have been.'

The pastor said, 'Be jealous of yourself, my Lord, but not of Jesus Christ, and know that there is no meeting betwixt Christ and you, except you be "weary and laden", for his commission from the Father (Isaiah 61:1–3) is only to the broken-hearted, to the captives, to the prisoners, and to the mourners in Zion.'

Whereupon [immediately after this] my Lord said with a deep sigh and with tears, 'God send me that!' and thereafter reckoned out a number of sins which, said he, are as serpents and crocodiles before my eyes. Thereafter my Lord said, 'But this hath been a sudden warning that God hath given me. What shall I do? I am afraid to die, and I can neither win [get] through death, nor about [around] it.'

The pastor said, 'My Lord, death and you are strangers; you have not made your acquaintance yet with death, I hope you will tell another tale of death ere all the play be ended, and you shall think death a sweet messenger, who is coming to fetch you up to your Father's house.'

Upon this he said with tears, 'God make it so,' and desired the pastor to pray.

ༀༀ

3

Anguish arising from impenitence —the third conversation with Rutherford

A T the third conference my Lord said, 'Death bindeth me strait. Oh how sweet a thing it is to seek God in health, and in time of prosperity to make our accounts! For now, through bodily pain, I am so distempered [unsettled] that I cannot get my heart framed to think upon my accounts, and the life to come!'

The pastor said, 'My Lord, it is a part of your battle to fight against sickness and pain, no less then [than] against sin and death, seeing sickness is a temptation.'

My Lord said, 'I have taken the play very long. God hath given me five and thirty years to repent (and alas I have misspent it) and now I see an ugly fight.' Then he covered his face with a linen cloth, and burst into tears and wept sore.

The pastor said, 'My Lord, they be far behind who may not follow. Think not your time so late: Christ's door is yet half open. You have time to throng [press] in, and your time is not all spent as yet. It is, I grant, far after noon, and the back of the day is now—yea the edge of your evening—but run fast, that ye lie not in the fields and miss your lodging.'

Upon that, my Lord said, with his eyes lifted up to heaven, 'Lord, how can I run? Lord, draw me, and I shall run.' (Song 1:4). The pastor, hearing that, desired him to pray, but he answered nothing. But within one hour after, he called for the pastor, and in the hearing of his Lady and him, he prayed divinely and graciously, with tears. The contents of his prayer were a bemoaning to God of his weak estate, both inward and outward, for, said he, 'Lord I am oppressed with pain without, sorrow and fear within. I dare not knock at thy door. I lie at it, but scraping as I may, till thou come out and take me in. I dare not speak. I look up to thee and wait on for a smack [taste] and kiss of Christ's fair face. Oh, when wilt thou come?'

ഹരു

4

A covenant with Christ
—the fourth conversation with
Rutherford

AT the fourth conference, he, calling for the pastor, said, 'I charge you: go to a secret place to God, and pray for me, and take help of others with you, and do it not for the fashion [pretence]. I know prayer will pull Christ out of heaven.'

The pastor said, 'My Lord, what shall we seek from God to you? Give us a commission from your own mouth.'

My Lord answered, 'I charge you to tell my beloved that I am sick of love.'

The pastor said, 'Shall we seek life and recovery to you?'

He answered, 'Yea, if it be God's good pleasure. For I find my fear of death now less, and I think God is loosing the roots of this deep-grown tree of my soul so strongly fastened to this life.'

The pastor said, 'My Lord, you must swear a covenant to God that, if he restore you to this life again, you shall renew your obedience to God, and that Jesus Christ shall be dearer to your soul than your honours, pleasures, credit, place, baronies[10] and lands, and all that you have.'

He said ere the pastor had ended, 'I trow [trust] so, and all too little for him. And by God's grace I bind myself under the pain of everlasting wrath to bide [abide] by that covenant, if the Lord should restore me.'

The pastor said, 'My Lord, our hearts are deceitful above all things. See that you be honest and stedfast to Jesus Christ in your covenant.' Then he read to him the 78th Psalm, 36th verse, of a false covenant that men often make under heavy troubles, and verse 34, 'When he slew them, then they sought him: and they returned, and enquired early after God,' and verse 35, 'And they remembered that God was their rock, and the high God their redeemer,' and verse 36, 'Nevertheless they did flatter him with their mouth, and they lied unto him with their tongues,' and verse 37, 'For their heart was not right with him, neither were they steadfast in his covenant.'

My Lord said, when he heard this read, 'In despite of the devil, that's not my covenant.'

My Lord took the Bible, and said, 'Mark other Scriptures for me to read,' and he marked to him the 2 Corinthians 5; Revelation 21; Revelation 22; Isaiah 38; Psalm 38; John 14.

These places he turned over, and cried frequently, 'Lord, for one of thy love-blinks [affectionate looks]; O Son of God, one sight of thy face!'

---

[10] Estates created by direct grant from the Crown.

The pastor said, 'My Lord, your prayers and your tears are come up before God, and Christ hath obtained a pardon for you.'

My Lord took the pastor by the hand and drew him to him, and said with a sigh and tears, 'Good news indeed!' Thereafter he called the pastor and convened such as went with him to pray for him, and said, 'Have you gotten any heavenly liberty and access to God in Christ for my soul?' They said they had, and he rejoiced, and said, 'Then I will believe and wait on. I cannot think but my beloved is coming, leaping over the mountains and skipping over the hills.'

When any friends or others came to visit him, whom he knew to fear God, he said at the first, 'Go try your power with God for me: go and pray.' He sent two of them at their first coming to him to the wood of the Kenmure, expressly to pray for him. After some cool of a fever (as was thought) he said to a gentlewoman who was a good Christian, who at his own desire attended him continually, 'Marion,[11] I desire one word of the pastor,' who, being called, came, to whom he said smiling, 'Joy now, for he is come! Oh, if I had a tongue to tell the world what Jesus Christ hath done to my soul!'

₮)℞

---

[11] Marion M'Naught, daughter to the Laird of Kilquhanidy, the representative of an ancient family (now extinct), connected at a remote date by marriage with the house of Kenmure, was wife of William Fullerton, Provost of Kirkcudbright. She was a woman of exemplary piety, and known to the most eminent clergymen and Christians of her day. 'Blessed be the Lord,' says Rutherford, 'that in God's mercy I found in this country such a woman, to whom Christ is dearer than her own heart, when there be so many that cast him over their shoulders.' [Footnote from 1828 edition]

5

Coldness and unconfessed sin
—the fifth conversation with Rutherford

BUT after this, my Lord, conceiving hope of recovery, became exceeding careless, remiss and dead, and seldom called for the pastor. For the space of two days he continued so, hoping to recover, howbeit upon no terms he would permit the pastor to go home to his kirk and flock till the Lord's Day was passed. This coldness gave occasion—to my Lady and the pastor, and other his friends and lovers—of heaviness, seeing his care for his soul so exceedingly slacked [diminished].

This made the pastor go to the physician, and asked his judgment for his life, who answered plainly that there was nothing for him but death, which would be certain if his flux [discharge of blood] returned, which in effect did return. This made the pastor go in to him, and say, 'My Lord, I have a necessary business to impart unto you,' and he said, 'Say on.'

'My Lord, you are not aware of a deep and fearful temptation of the devil, by which your soul is dangerously ensnared? You have conceived hope to return back again to this life, but I tell you, my Lord, ere it be long, you shall be presented before the Judge of quick [living] and dead, to receive doom [judgment] and sentence according to your works. I have warrant for me to say this; therefore I beseech you, my Lord, as you tender [value] your own soul's salvation, be not deceived ere it be long. Time will be no more with you; eternity is drawing on. Your glass [hourglass] is shorter then [than] you are aware of. Satan would be glad to steal your soul out of this life sleeping.'

The physician likewise seconded these speeches, and faithfully gave him warning of the danger of his disease, and told him for the salvation of his soul, it was his wisdom to be prepared, and told him plainly that he thought his time should not be long.

After these words, he took the pastor by the hand and said that he 'found faithful and plain dealing. This man and I will not sunder [part] till death sunder us. Now I will set aside all things. I know one thing is needful. It was but the folly of my deceiving heart, to look back over my shoulder to this life, when I was fairly [well] on once in my journey towards heaven.' And therefore he caused all men to go out of the chamber, save only the pastor, and caused him close the doors and confer with him anent [concerning] the state of his soul.

The pastor, after prayer, said, 'My Lord, I perceive I have been deceived and your Lordship also, for your joy I fear hath not been well-rooted, neither your humiliation so deep as need were. We must dig deeper again, and seek a lower foundation, for when I bethink me [come to think] of your coldness in devotion and your untimeous [inopportune] relenting in the necessary work of making your reckoning with your Judge, upon vain conceived hope of recovery of health, I see certainly the work is not sure: one pin[12] is loose. Your Lordship knoweth this church and country hath been grievously offended at many gross and open sins in you, both against the first and second table of the law.'

And upon this the pastor burdened him with sundry particulars, and told him plainly, and said, 'My Lord, my mistake of the case of your soul hath been from hence, that you have never cleared yourself of many predominant and bosom sins, whereof I both spoke and writ [wrote] to you. And you may remember how malcontent you were at a sharp letter of many particulars that I writ to your Lordship, and how at your house of Rusco [Rusco Castle, Gatehouse of Fleet] you made half a challenge of it to me—for I found you always witty [shrewd] to shift [evade] and cover any thing whereof you were rebuked. Howbeit, at my first coming to this country, when you sided too much with a gentleman of your name who killed a man vilely, you promised willingly to receive and take in good part what I freely told your Lordship was amiss.'[13]

Whereupon my Lord reckoned [counted] out a number of fearful sins, which because Jesus Christ hath covered, the pastor will never discover [uncover]. But amongst all, he ingenuously and freely confessed his sin in deserting the last parliament, and said, 'God knoweth I did it with the fearful wrestlings of my conscience, my light [spiritual illumination] paying me home within [chastising me inwardly], when I

---

[12] A piece of wood or metal holding a structure together.
[13] This paragraph affords a decisive proof that it was Rutherford who attended Kenmure on this mournful occasion. It exhibits, moreover, an interesting example of the unbending and conscientious manner in which he performed his professional duties, without distinction of rank or of individuals. [Footnote from 1828 edition]

seemed to be glad and joyful before men. Yet I did it for fear of incurring the indignation of my Prince, and the loss of farther honour, which I certainly expected. But woe, woe be to honours or anything else bought with the loss of peace of conscience and God's favour.'

The pastor being struck with fear and astonishment at the reckoning [numbering] of those fearful sins (which my Lord had kept close, notwithstanding of such fair appearance of a sound mark of grace in his soul as he had conceived), did then stand up and read unto him the first eight verses of the 6th to the Hebrews, and discoursed to him of the far on-going [progress] of reprobates in the way of heaven, and of their taste of the good Word of God and of the virtues of the life to come, and yet are but reprobates, and cited also Revelation 21, 'But the fearful and unbelievers, and the abominable murderers, whoremongers, etc. shall have their part in the lake that burneth with fire and brimstone, which is the second death,' and told him what everlasting burning was. And with that the pastor turned his back upon him, and said, 'Now, my Lord, I have not one word of mercy from my Lord to say to you. God hath sealed up my lips that I dare speak nothing to you but one thing—the wrath and ire of God Almighty.'

My Lord hearing this, with tears cried out so that they heard him in the withdrawing room[14] and in all the houses about. Then he said, 'God armed in wrath is coming against me, to beat out my brains. I would [wish to] die, I would not die; I

---

[14] A room to which the owners of the house and distinguished visitors could 'withdraw' for more privacy. It was often off the great chamber. Later, the name changed to 'drawing room'.

dare not live. Oh what a burden is the hand of an angry God! Oh, what shall I do? Is there no hope of mercy?'

Thus in a fearful agony he lay a long time weeping, so that those who attended broke in and said the pastor had no skill, he would kill him, and others said, 'I pray you beware, you will not fail to thrust him into despair.' The pastor, not content with those speeches, did bear with them, and went to a quiet part, and sought from God his salvation and words from God to speak to this patient. And some said that the pastor was a miserable comforter.

After this, another pastor came to visit my Lord, to whom my Lord said, 'He hath slain me.' And before the pastor could speak for himself, my Lord said, 'Not he hath slain me, but the spirit of God in him.'

The pastor said, 'Not I, but the law hath slain you. And, my Lord, I say yet again, the God of heaven hath a terrible process [lawsuit] against your father's house, and a deep and a bloody controversy with the stones and the timber of the house of Kenmure. And, my Lord, your name is in the process. See how you can free yourself; God is not mocked.'

The other brother read to him the history of Manasseh's most wicked life, and how the Lord was entreated of him and gave him mercy, but the former pastor went still upon wrath and asked of him, saying, 'My Lord, you are extremely pained, I know, now both in body and mind. What think you of the lake of fire and brimstone, of everlasting burnings, and of utter darkness with the devil and his angels?'

My Lord said, 'Woe is me! What can I think of it? I think if I should suffer my thoughts to dwell upon it any space, it were enough to cause me go out of my wits. But I pray you, man, what shall my soul do?'

The pastor answered, 'My Lord, I am where I was. God knoweth I dissemble not. I have not one word of mercy to speak to you. Only I know Christ hath not given out the doom against you, the sentence is yet suspended; therefore mourn and sorrow for the offending of your God.'

The pastor said, 'What, my Lord, if Christ had given out a sentence of condemnation, and come to your bedside and told you of it? Would you not still love him, and trust in him and hang upon him?'

My Lord said, 'God knoweth I durst [dare] not challenge him. Yea, howbeit he should not love me, yet I will still love him. Yea though the Lord should slay me, yet I will trust in him. I will lie down at God's feet. Let him trample upon me; I will die if I die [might die] at Christ's feet.'

The pastor finding my Lord claiming kindness to Christ, and hearing him cry often, 'O Son of God, where art thou? When wilt thou come to me? Oh for a love look!' then the pastor said, 'Is it possible, my Lord, that you can love and long for Christ, and he not love and long for you? Or can love and kindness stand only upon your side? Is your poor, feckless [feeble], unworthy love greater than infinite love, seeing he hath said (Isaiah 49:15), "Can a woman forget her sucking child, that she should not have compassion on the son of her womb? Yea, they may forget, yet will I not forget thee"? Verse 16: "Behold, I have graven thee upon the palms of my hands," etc., and therefore your loving and longing for Christ is a fire of God's kindling. My Lord, persuade yourself, you are graven on the palms of God's hands.'

Upon this my Lord, with a hearty smile, looked about to a gentleman, a good Christian, whom he had commanded to attend his body till his dying hour. 'Man,' saith my Lord, 'I am written upon the palms of Christ's hands; he will not forget me. Is not this brave talking?'

The pastor, finding him weaker, said, 'My Lord, the marriage day is drawing near. Make ready the marriage robes. Set aside all care of your estate and the world, and give yourself to meditation, prayer, and spiritual conference.'

He was observed after that to be always upon that exercise and, when none was near him, he was overheard praying, and many times when, to our sense, he was sound sleeping, he was at prayer.

℘℃

6

Reconciliation with adversaries

AFTER a sleep he called for the pastor and said, 'I have been troubled in my sleep with this, that being at peace with God, I am not also at peace with men, and therefore send for such a kinsman (with whom I am not reconciled) as also for a minister that had before offended me, that I may friend [be reconciled] with them,' which was done quickly.

When the preacher came, he said, 'I have ground of offence against you as a natural man, and now I do to you what all men breathing could not have moved me to do. But now, because the Holy Spirit commands me, I must obey, and therefore I freely forgive you, as I would wish you to forgive me. You are in an eminent [conspicuous] place. Walk before God and be faithful in your calling, and take heed to your steps, walk in the right road, hold your eye right. For all the world, decline not [do not deviate] from holiness, and take example by me.'

To his cousin he said, 'Serve the Lord, and follow not the footsteps of your father-in-law'—he had married the Bishop of Galloway's daughter. 'Learn to know that you have a soul, for I say to you the thousandth part of the world knoweth not they have a soul; the world liveth without any sense of God.'

He willed the pastor to sleep in a bed made upon the ground beside himself within the chamber, and urged him against his will to lie down and sleep, and said, 'You and I have a far journey to go; make you [make yourself ready] for it.'

૪૦૦૨

7

Rejoicing in Christ
—the sixth conversation with
Rutherford

SOME four nights before his death he would [wished to] drink a cup of wine to the pastor, who answered, 'I receive it, my Lord, in hope you shall drink of the pure river of water of life, proceeding from the throne of God, and from the Lamb.' And when the cup was in his hand, with a smiling countenance he said, 'I think I have good cause to drink with a good will to you.'

After some heaviness, the pastor said, 'My Lord, I come with news to you.'

He answered, 'What be they?'

The pastor answered, 'Be not afraid of death and judgment, because the process [lawsuit] that your Judge had against you is cancelled and rent in pieces, and Jesus Christ hath trampled it under his feet: your dittay [indictment] is burnt.'

My Lord said very pithily [forcefully] with a smile, 'Oh that is a luckie [blessed] tale. I will then believe and rejoice, for sure I am that Jesus Christ and I once met, and will he not come again?'

The pastor said, 'My Lord, you have gotten the firstfruits of the Spirit, the earnest, and Christ will not lose his earnest; therefore the bargain betwixt Christ and your soul holdeth.'

He asked the pastor, 'What is Christ like, that I may know him?'

The pastor answered, 'He is like love, and altogether lovely (Song 5:6). Love cannot but be known, wheresoever it is.'

The pastor said, 'My Lord, if you had the man Christ in your arms very now [right now], would you not thrust him to your heart, howbeit your breasts and side be pained with a stitch?'

He answered, 'God knoweth I would forget my pain, and thrust him into my heart. Yea, if I had my heart in the palm of my hand, I would give it him, and think it too unworthy a gift for him.'

He complained of Jesus Christ's going and coming. 'I find', said he, 'my soul drowned with heaviness. When the Lord cometh, he stayeth not long.'

The pastor said, 'Wooers dwell not together, but married folks take up house together and sunder [separate] not. Jesus Christ is now wooing, and therefore he feedeth his own with hunger, which is as growing meat, as the sense of his presence.'

He said often, 'Son of God, when wilt thou come? God is not as man that he should change, or as the son of man that he should repent; those that come to Christ, he casteth not away, but raiseth them up at the last day.' Still, after peace and full assurance of reconciliation, he cast back his eyes to his sins and mourned.

The pastor discoursed to him of the new Jerusalem and the glory of our Father's house up above, and said, 'What will you think, my Lord, when Christ shall dry your watery eyes, and wipe all tears from your face, and lay your head upon his breast, and embrace you in his arms, and kiss you with the kisses of his mouth?'

He said, 'I want [lack] words to say what I think, but I know heaven is above the commendation of all earthly men, howbeit they had the tongues of angels.'

He was heard to say in his sleep, 'My wellbeloved is mine, and I am his.' Being asked if he had been sleeping, he said he was asleep, but he remembered he was giving a claim to Christ in his sleep.

Another time, after sleep he wakened with exceeding great joy not long before his death, saying, 'I have felt an extreme sweetness, which did arise from the lower parts of my body and come up to my heart as sweet perfume, and so filled it that I was not able to contain the same, but as a precious perfume, it diffused itself through the whole rooms about me with a most delicate and odoriferous smell.' The doctor of physic [physician] desired him to say over [repeat] the words again, which he did, and said he felt joy unspeakable and glorious.

After a sound sleep in the dawning, the pastor said, 'My Lord, where lay Christ all night? Did not your wellbeloved lie as a bundle of myrrh betwixt your breasts?'

He answered, 'Nay, not betwixt my breasts, but within my breasts, locked in my heart.'

He asked, 'When will my heart be loosed and my tongue untied, that I may express the sweetness of the law of God to my own soul?' And before the pastor answered anything, he answered himself, 'Even when the wind bloweth.'

Being asked by the pastor if ever he had benefitted by the Word of God in public, which he had heard preached these many years, he answered, 'I never came to your communion but I was filled with the sense of God, and Christ was powerfully borne in upon my soul that, do my best, I was not able to hold him out [exclude him], but in would he be, whether I would [wished it] or not. But oh, oh, my woeful outbreakings for the sins I was inclined to! The devil and temptations took me at such a nick [deceit] as I could not win by [get the victory] unhurt. But oh, strong, strong Jesus! Oh the deep [depth] of his love that would not want [fail] me!'

Being asked what was his judgment anent the ceremonies now entered into the Kirk of God, he answered, 'I think and am persuaded in my conscience they are superstitious, idolatrous and antichristian, and come from hell. And I repute it a mercy that my eyes shall not see the desolation that shall come upon this poor church. It is plain Popery that is coming among you. God help you! God forgive the nobility, for they are either key-cold, or ready to welcome Popery, whereas they should resist. And woe be to a dead, time-serving and profane ministry; they are but a company of dumb dogs.'

ഗ്രര

8

Kenmure's advice
from the border of eternity

HE called his Lady, and a gentleman who was a friend to
his Lady and had come from the east country a good
way to visit him with the pastor.

He caused shut the chamber door upon all others, and from
his bed directed his speech to the gentleman, saying, 'I ever
did find you kind and honest to me all the time of my life.
Therefore I must now give you a charge, which you shall
deliver to all the noblemen you know, and with whom you
are acquainted. Go through them and tell them all how heavy
I have found the weight of the Lord's hand upon me for not
giving testimony for the Lord my God, when I had occasion
once in my life at the last parliament. For this foul fault, how
fierce have I felt the wrath of the Lord my God! My soul hath
raged and roared. I have been ripped up [grieved] to the heart.

'Tell them that they will be as I am now. Encourage others
that stood for the Lord. Tell them that failed, that as ever they
would wish to have mercy when they are as I am now, that
they would repent and crave mercy from God. Would to God

I had such an occasion again to testify my love to the Lord! For all the earth should I not do as I have done, tell them.'

༄༅

To a gentleman, a kinsman of his,[15] he said, 'I love your soul and I love your body. You are a blessed man if you understand it, because ye may have the blessed means of the Word preached beside you. And seeing you are but a tender man of body, I would not have you to drown yourself so much with trysting and fasheries [meetings and troubles] of this world (as I did); who knows but you may be the first man [that] may follow me [into the grave].

'My greatest grief is that I had not the occasion of good means as you have, and if you yourself make not the right use of the occasion of your means, one day they shall be a witness against you. Alas, take example by me! I was a fool and lifted up with folly, and now when I was at the very top, I was taken by the Lord, when I expected least. The Lord hath smitten me, therefore take example by me, and leave the world and the fasheries of friends timeously [promptly].

'Tender [offer] your soul, and tender your worn body. If I were to live in the world again, I should not vex and fash [trouble] myself so much as I did, but should dwell at the Rusco the most part of my life, that I might have the happiness of the exercise of hearing God's Word preached [at

---

[15] The kinsman here spoken of was, I think, John Gordon of Cardoness in the parish of Anwoth, a man of great piety and a zealous supporter of the Presbyterian faith. We find his son who, with the father, were regular correspondents of Rutherford, in the covenanting army in England in 1644. [Footnote from 1828 edition]

Anwoth] as you have, good cousin. Use the counsel of your pastor.'

ℰℭ

To a Lord that was his brother-in-law:[16] 'Mock not at my counsel, my Lord. In case [If] you follow the course you are in, you shall never see the face of Jesus Christ; you are deceived with the merchandise of the whore that makes the world drunk out of the cup of her fornications. Your soul is built upon a sandy foundation. When you come to my estate, you will find no comfort in your religion. You know not what wrestlings I have had before I came to this estate of comfort. The kingdom of heaven is not gotten with a skip or leap, but with much seeking, thrumbling [struggling] and thrusting.

My Lord Herries, not liking this discourse, did press to break it off by these words, saying, 'My Lord, I thank you kindly, I am content to see your Lordship so resolved. If I had known of your Lordship's sickness, I had seen you sooner.'

My Lord Kenmure answered, 'I pray God give you grace to make good use of your coming. Seeing you are now come, contemn [despise] not good counsel, for I have interest in your Lordship and love your soul, and I must exoner [exonerate] myself as I will be answerable to God.'

ℰℭ

To a Lady that was his own sister: 'Who knows, sister, if the words of a dying brother may prevail with a living sister. Alas!

---

[16] John Maxwell, 7th Lord Herries of Terregles, a Roman Catholic. He later became the 3rd Earl of Nithsdale.

You incline to a rotten religion.[17] Fie, cast away these rotten dregs! They will not avail you when you are brought to this case as I am. The half of the world is ignorant and goeth to hell, and knoweth not that they have a soul. It is a wonder to see any to know that they have a soul. Read the Scriptures! They are plain Scottish language to all who desire wisdom from God and to be led to heaven.'

ဢၐ

To a gentleman his neighbour: 'Your soul is in a dangerous case, but you see it not. And as long as you are in the case you are in, you will never see it. I pray you, as you love the salvation of your soul, leave these courses: you must seek out another way to heaven then [than] you are in, else look to land at hell. There are small means of instruction to be had, because the most part of the ministry are profane and ignorant. Search God's Word for the good old way, and search and find [out the error of] all your own ways.'

ဢၐ

To a gentleman his cousin, he said, 'You are a young man, and knowest not well what you are doing. Seek God's direction for wisdom in your affairs and you shall prosper, and learn to know you have need of God to be your friend.'

ဢၐ

To another cousin: 'David, you are an aged man, and you know not well what an account you have to make. And if you

---

[17] The sister is not named. In chapter 8, it is recorded that Lady Herries (his sister) was a Roman Catholic.

were in the case I am in, you would count more of your accounts then [than] you do. I know you better then [than] you believe, for you worship God according to man's devices. You believe lies of [about] God; your soul is in a fearful case. And while [until] you know the truth you shall never see your own way aright.'

ఠఙ

To a young man, his neighbour: 'Because you are but a young man, beware of temptations and snares. And above all, be careful to keep yourself in the use of means, resort to good company. And howbeit you be nicknamed a Puritan[18] and mocked, yet care not for that, but rejoice and be glad that they who are scorned and scoffed by this godless and vain world, and nicknamed Puritans, would admit you to their society, for I must tell you when I am at this point as you see me, I get no comfort to my soul by any second means under heaven but from these who are nicknamed Puritans. They are the men that can give a word of comfort to a wearied soul in due sea-

---

[18] It must be remembered that the Puritans were a movement in the Church in England, not in Scotland. Whilst the Puritans shared some common ground with the Scottish Presbyterians, the two groups were entirely distinct. The Scottish Episcopalians used 'Puritan' as a term of abuse for the Covenanters, who refused to conform to the imposed ceremonies. Rutherford consistently wrote the word 'Puritan' only in allusion to the term of abuse applied by enemies to godliness (see *Letters* 11, 59 and 262, as well as the present instance).
It is nowadays a common mistake to refer to the Covenanters as either Puritans or Scottish Puritans. However, they never described themselves as Puritans, and George Gillespie considered it reprehensible to be labelled with this reproach for faithfulness to God's truth (see *Dispute against the English Popish Ceremonies* in Gillespie's *Works*, vol. 1, p. 39).

son, and that I have found by experience since I did lie down here.'

℘℘

To one of his natural [illegitimate] sisters: 'My dove, thou art young and, alas, ignorant of God. I know thy breeding and thine upbringing well enough: seek the Spirit of regeneration! Oh, if thou knew it and felt the power of that Spirit as I do now, think not all is gone because your brother is dead! Trust in God, and your Father liveth,[19] and beware of the follies of youth. Give yourself to reading and praying and careful hearing of God's Word, and take heed whom you hear and how you hear. God be with you!'

℘℘

To another pastor, Mr. James [Irving of Parton]:[20] 'It is not holiness enough to be a minister, for you ministers have your own faults, and those more heinous then [than] other. I pray you be more painful [assiduous] in your calling and take good heed to the flock of God. And know that every soul that perisheth by your negligence shall be counted to you soul-murderers before God. Think not but such a man as I may at this time give a wise man counsel. Take heed in these

---

[19] Their father died in 1628. It is likely Kenmure meant that God would be a father to her.
[20] Mr Irving, soon after this time, inclined to Episcopal principles, and took part with Bishop Sydserf in his persecution of the Presbyterians. On the downfall of Episcopacy, however, in 1638, he resumed his original faith, and continued in the charge of Parton. [Footnote from 1828 edition]

dangerous days how you lead the people of God, and take heed to your ministry.'

℘℞

To his chaplain, who then was Mr George Gillespie:[21] 'You have carried yourself discreetly to me, so that I cannot blame you. I hope you shall prove an honest man. If I have been at any times harsh to you, forgive me, I would [wish] I had taken better heed to many of your words. I might have gotten good by the means that God gave me, but I made no use of them. Now I see it was God [who] sent this pastor unto me, because he resolved to stay longer at Irvine. The Lord hath now let me see my ways. My soul hath been troubled for them, but my God hath given me comfort and hath begun to loosen my tongue. God be thanked for that which I have gotten, I look for more. Great is the work of mercy that is shown to me now! The love of God is made known to my soul, and I am grieved for my ingratitude against my loving Lord and that I should have sinned against him, who came down from the heaven to the earth for my cause, to die for my sins. The sense of this love, borne in upon my heart, hath a reflex making me love my Saviour and grip to him back again. The sparks and

---

[21] Mr Gillespie was afterwards minister of Wemyss [Fife], and subsequently one of the ministers of Edinburgh. He was so eminent as to be appointed one of the commissioners from the Church of Scotland to the Assembly of Divines at Westminster, and Moderator of the General Assembly [of the Church] in 1648, towards the end of which year he died in the prime of his life. He was the author of various works, of which the *Dispute against the English Popish ceremonies obtruded upon the Church of Scotland* (Edinburgh, 1637) is the most celebrated. [Footnote from 1828 edition]

flaughens [flames] of this love shall fly up and down this bed, so long as I lie in it.'

୫୨୦୪

To another kinsman he said: 'Learn to use your precious time well. Oh, alas! The ministry in this country is dead. God help you! Ye are not rightly led: ye have need to be busy among yourselves. And the knowledge God hath given you, use it and practise it. Men are as careless in the practice of godliness, as if godliness were nothing but fashious [vexatious] words, sighs and shows. But all these will not do the turn. Oh but I find it now hard, to take heaven by violence and to thrust in at.'

୫୨୦୪

To two gentlemen neighbours: 'It is not rising soon in the morning and running out to the park[22] and stone-ditch that will bring peace to the conscience when it comes to this part of the play. You know not how I have been beguiled with the world. I would counsel you to seek that one thing that is necessary, even the salvation of your soul. Be continually casting [going over] your accounts; let not your reckonings be behind as mine were, but count [reckon] with your own souls every day and every night.'

୫୨୦୪

---

[22] Enclosed land, either as a garden or for the purpose of hunting.

To a cousin [Robert Gordon], Bailie[23] of Ayr: 'Robert, I know you have light and understanding. And though you have no need to be instructed by me, yet have you need to be incited. Care not over much for the world, but make use of the good occasions and means you have in your country, for here is a pack of dumb dogs that cannot bark. They tell over [recount] a clash of terror and a clatter of comfort, without any sense or life.'

ಬಿಂಕ

To a young cousin, and another young gentleman that was his friend: 'Sirs, ye are young men, and ye have far to go. And it may be some of you have not far to go. And if it fall out that your journey be short, howsoever it is dangerous, now are you happy because you have time to lay [reckon up] your accounts with Jesus Christ. See, therefore, that your reckoning be made daily, lest you be taken (as I am) to make your accounts, and to have all your senses to seek about you.[24] Suffer not, therefore, this example that you see of me to slip unobserved, but make your best use of it. I entreat you to give your youth to Jesus Christ, for it is the most precious offer and acceptable gift you can give him. Give not your youth to the devil and your lusts, and then reserve nothing to Jesus Christ but your old rotten bones. It is to be feared that then he will not accept you. Learn therefore to watch and take example by me.'

ಬಿಂಕ

---

[23] Municipal officer or magistrate.
[24] The sense appears to be: 'to be aware of what is going on around you'.

He called Bishop Lamb,[25] who was then Bishop of Galloway, commanding all who were within the chamber to remove [leave the room], and had with him a long conference.

He exhorted him most earnestly not to molest or remove the Lord's servants, and not to enforce or enthral their consciences to receive the Five Articles of Perth,[26] nor to do anything against their consciences, but to behave himself meekly toward them as he would wish to have mercy from God.

The bishop answered, 'My Lord, our ceremonies are of their own nature but things indifferent, and we impose them for decency and order in God's kirk. They need not to stand scrupulously upon them as matters of conscience in God's worship.'

---

[25] Andrew Lamb was translated [moved, as a clergyman] from the See of Brechin to that of Galloway in 1619, on the death of Bishop Cowper. Though a member of the High Commission and though in consequence concurring in the propriety and necessity of that institution, he manifested in his own diocese forbearance and toleration which cannot be too highly praised. He died in less than three months after Kenmure, and was succeeded by Sydserf, a man of a totally opposite character. [Footnote from 1828 edition]

[26] The Five Articles of Perth were devised by King James VI to impose episcopalian practices on the Church of Scotland. They were introduced at a General Assembly in that town in 1618. The articles required kneeling (rather than sitting) when partaking of the Lord's Supper, private communion, baptism not withheld longer than one Sabbath after birth (and administered in private where necessary), the rite of confirmation by a bishop, and the observance of 'holy days' such as 'Christmas' and 'Easter'. David Dickson and George Gillespie were notable opponents of the Perth articles. Their writings prepared the way for the Glasgow Assembly of 1638, which condemned the Perth Assembly as null and repealed each of the articles.

64

My Lord Kenmure replied, 'I am not to dispute with you, but one thing I know, and can tell you out of dear experience, that these things indeed are matters of conscience, and not indifferent. And so I have found them, for since I did lie down in this bed, the sin that lieth heaviest upon my soul and hath burdened my conscience most, was my withdrawing of myself from the parliament and not giving my voice for the truth against these things that they call indifferent, for in so doing I have denied the Lord my God.'

When the bishop began to commend and encourage him for his well-led life, and did put him in hope of health, and praised him for his civil carriage [conduct] and legal [law-abiding] behaviour, saying he was not an oppressor, and without any known vice, he answered, 'My Lord, that's no matter. A man may be a good civil neighbour, and yet go to hell.'

The bishop answered, 'I confess, my Lord, we have all our own faults,' and thereafter insisted [persisted] in long discourse, that my Lord thought impertinent [not pertinent].

This made him interrupt the bishop, saying, 'What should I more? I have gotten a grip of Jesus Christ, and Christ of me. God be with your Lordship!'

On the morrow the bishop come to visit him and said, 'My Lord, how do you?'

My Lord answered, 'I thank God, as well as a saved man hastening to heaven can do.'

ℰℭ

After he had given the Clerk of Kirkcudbright a most divine and grave counsel anent his Christian carriage and how he should walk in his particular calling, he caused him hold up his hand and swear by the Lord that he should never consent but to oppose to the election of a corrupt minister or magistrate.

೫ (೪

He said to his coachman: 'You will now go to any man that will give you most hire [wages]. But do not so. Go where ye may get best company. Though you get less wages, yet will you get the more grace because your calling [occupation] is subject to drunkenness and company [worldly companionship].' (He made him hold up his hand and promise before God to do so.)

೫ (೪

To two young serving men that came to him weeping to get his last blessing, he said, 'Content not yourselves to be like old wives with a superficial show of religion, to make a show of blessing yourselves in the morning for the fashion [appearance] only. Yea, although you would pray both morning and evening, yet that will not avail you, except likewise you make your account every day. Oh, you will find few to direct or counsel you, but I will tell you what to do: first pray the Lord fervently to enlighten the eyes of your mind, then seek grace to rule your affections. You will find the good of this when you are as I am.'

He took their oath to strive to do so and, as he counselled them, he made many divine and powerful exhortations to so many sundry persons, that all might be hardly [with great difficulty] written for length. He caused every man to hold up their hands, and swear in his presence that, by God's grace, they should forbear their former sins, and follow his counsel.

ℰℛ

After he had exhorted many friends and servants, as they were going out of the chamber, he said to them, 'Stay, sirs. I have somewhat yet to say. Be not deceived with the world. As for me, I have played the fool and brought the house of Kenmure to the perfection of a complete fabric [structure] as it was never before, and busied myself exceedingly. And when I came to the top of my hopes, and thought to enjoy them, the Lord came and plucked me from my hopes. Thereafter I did see my own folly, and this also I observed in my father. Take example by me, and be not ensnared with the world. There be some who seek the world too carefully, and some too greedily, and many unlawfully. And men have it so much in their mind that they are upon the world in the morning, ere they come out of their bed, and before ever they seek God. Sirs, set your hearts to give pains [great care] in sad earnest for the kingdom of heaven. I will tell you, the heavenly kingdom is not gotten with a skip or a leap. I find it now, there must be thrusting and thronging [pressing] and climbing to enter in. It is a strait and narrow way.'

His omission of prayer in the morning time, through needless foils and distractions, touched his conscience. This he confessed with regret.

ℰℛ

He was giving a divine counsel to a friend, and rested in the midst of it, and looked up to heaven, and prayed for a loosed heart and tongue to express the goodness of God to men. And thereafter went on in his counsel, not unlike to Jacob (Genesis 49:18) who, in the midst of a prophetical testament, resteth a little and saith, 'Lord, I have waited for thy salvation.'

ℰᏩ

He gave his Lady diverse times (and that openly) an honourable and ample testimony of [her] holiness and goodness and all respective [attentive] kindness to her husband, and craved her forgiveness earnestly where he had offended her, and desired her to make the Lord her comforter, and said he was but gone before [he had preceded her in doing that], and it was but fifteen or sixteen years up or down [approximately].

ℰᏩ

He spoke ordinarily [one by one] to all the boys of the house, servants, butlers, cooks, omitting none, saying, 'Learn to serve and fear the Lord, and use the means of your salvation carefully, that you put not off your accounts to the hinder end of the day as I did foolishly. I know what is ordinarily your religion: ye go to the kirk, and when ye hear the devil or hell named in the preaching, ye sigh and make a noise, and it is forgot [forgotten] with you before you come home, and then ye are holy enough. But I can now tell you the kingdom of heaven is not gotten so easily. Then your pastors and guides mislead you. They are but a pack of dumb dogs. Use the means yourself and win to [get] some sense of God, and pray as you can, morning and evening. If you be ignorant of the way to heaven, God forgive you, for I discharge myself in that point toward you, and appointed a man [Mr George Gillespie] to teach you: your blood be upon yourselves. The little knowledge that you have, if you would use it carefully and with a good conscience, the Lord would lead you on farther, and teach you his ways. But your form is to ask for that master who will give you most hire [wages], and little care you to live in good company where you may find the means of salvation. And so ye spend the time all over in the ignorance of God.'

၄ၢ

He took an oath of [from] his servants that they should follow his advice. He had a speech severally [individually] to every one of them. He was so far humbled that he said to every one of them (the meanest not excepted), 'If I have been rough to thee, or offended thee, I pray thee for God's sake forgive me.'

And among others, one to whom he had been rough, said, 'Your Lordship did me never wrong. I will never get such a master again.' Yet my Lord urged the boy to say, 'My Lord, I forgive you,' howbeit the boy was hardly [with great difficulty] brought to utter these words.

၄ၢ

He said to all the beholders about him, 'Sirs, behold how low the Lord hath laid me.'

၄ၢ

To a gentleman burdened in his estate, 'Sir, I counsel you to cast your burdens upon the Lord your God.'

၄ၢ

A worthy and religious gentleman of his name[27] came to visit him four days before his death. He beholding him afar off said, 'Robert, come to me. Leave me not till I die.' Thereafter being much comforted with the gentleman's words, he would have him to wait upon his body, and being more and more comforted with his speeches, he said, 'Robert, you are a friend, both to my soul and to my body.'

This gentleman asked him, saying, 'My Lord, what comfort has your soul in your love towards the saints?' He answered, 'I rejoice at it.'

Then he asked, 'What comfort have you in bringing this pastor who attends you to Galloway?'

He answered, 'God knoweth that I rejoice that ever God did put it in my heart so to do, and now because I aimed at God's glory in it, the Lord hath made me to find comfort to my soul. In the end, I would counsel all men, that think to die, to lay

---

[27] The individual spoken of in the text is, I think, Robert Gordon of Knockbrex. John Livingstone describes him as 'a simple-hearted and painful [diligent] Christian' who assisted the Covenanting cause after 1638. His name is well known to those acquainted with the history of Rutherford and his Letters. His grandnephews, John Gordon of Knockbrex and Robert Gordon, with Major John M'Culloch of Barholm and seven others, were executed at Edinburgh on the 7th December 1666 for having participated in the Pentland Rising that was terminated by the Battle of Rullion Green. They were grandsons of another of Rutherford's correspondents, Alexander Gordon of Garloch. Robert Wodrow says that they 'were youths of shining piety, and good learning and parts [intellect]. ... When Knockbrex and his brother were turned off the [gallows] ladder, they clasped one another in their arms, and thus endured the pangs of death.' (Wodrow's History). [Footnote from 1828 edition, with amendments]

up many good works against the time of departure. The ministers of Galloway murdered my father's soul,[28] and if this man had not come they had [would have] murdered mine also.'[29]

෪ඤ

In the hearing of my Lady Herries, his sister,[30] a Papist, he testified how willing he was to leave the world, that he could not command his soul to look back again to this life. He did so long (as he said) for his soulful of the well of life, that Papists may see that these who die in this religion, see and know well whither they go, and that we are by death fully loosed from the love of this world, for the hope of our own Father's house.

෪ඤ

It was told him that letters were come from some of his friends to him. He caused deliver them to his Lady, saying, 'I have nothing to do with them. I had rather hear of news from heaven concerning my eternal salvation.'

෪ඤ

---

[28] They gave his father a false hope for eternity.

[29] Kenmure, in the prospect of death, seems to have experienced great comfort from the recollection of having been the means of bringing a gospel and faithful clergyman like Rutherford to Anwoth. Kenmure previously alluded to the same circumstance end of chapter 1], and evidently appealed to it as the most meritorious action of his life.

[30] Elizabeth Gordon. In 1621, she married John Maxwell, 7th Lord Herries of Terregles.

It was observed, when any came to him anent worldly business, that before they were out at the doors, he returned unto praying, conference, meditation, or some spiritual exercise, and was exceeding short [hurried] in dispatching all earthly business; yet so as he took the pains to sign all needful writs [documents] when he was required. Likewise he recommended the case of the poor to his friends.

ℰᏮ

When he was wearing weaker, he fell in a swoon, and being awaked, he said with smiling and signs of joy to all about him, 'I would not exchange my life with you all—nay, not with you who are ministers. I feel the smell of the place where I am going to.'

ℰᏮ

9

Passing from time to eternity —the final conversation with Rutherford

UPON the Friday, in the morning, 12th September, which was the day of his departure, he said to the pastor, 'This night must I sup with Jesus Christ in paradise.'

The pastor read to him 2 Corinthians 5 and Revelation 22, and made some short notes [comments] upon such places as concerned his estate [condition]. After prayer he said, 'I conceive good hope that God looketh upon me when he gives his servants such liberty as to pray for me. Is it possible that Jesus Christ can loose his grips of me? Neither may my soul get itself plucked from Jesus Christ.'

He earnestly desired sense of God's presence, and the pastor said, 'What, my Lord, if that be suspended till you come to your own home, and be before the throne clothed in white, and get your harp in your hand to sing salvation to the Lamb, and to him that sitteth on the throne? For that is heaven, and who dare promise you it upon earth? There is a piece of nature in desiring a sense of God's love, it being an apple that the Lord's children delight to play with. But, my Lord, if you would have it only as a pledge of your salvation, we shall seek it from the Lord to you, and you may lawfully pray for it.' Earnest prayers were made for him, and my Lord testified that he was filled with the sense of his Lord's love.

Being asked what he thought of the world, he answered, 'It is bitterer than gall or wormwood.' Being demanded [asked] if now he feared death, he answered, 'I have tasted death now. It is not a whit bitter. Welcome the messenger of Jesus Christ.' He never left off to mourn for his sins, especially his deserting of the parliament.

The pastor said to him, 'My Lord, there is a process [lawsuit] betwixt the Lord and your father's house, but your name is taken out of the process. Dear (and how dear!) was heaven bought for you by your Saviour Jesus Christ.'

'I know there is wrath against my father's house, but I shall get my soul for a prey,' which words he had frequently in his mouth. Oft-times also he would say, 'Is not this a sweet word that God saith, "As I live, I delight not in the death of sinners"?' He said often, 'I will not let go the grip that I have gotten of Christ. Though he should slay me I will trust in him, and lie at his feet and die there, and lie at his door like a beggar waiting on, and if I may not knock, I shall scrape.' Another word was ordinary [frequent] to him, 'O Son of God, one love-blink [affectionate look], one smack [taste], one kiss of thy mouth, one smile.'

When he had been deep in a meditation of his change of life [his death], he made this question, 'What will Jesus Christ be like when he cometh?' It was answered, 'All lovely.'

The day of his change, being Friday 12ᵗʰ September, he was heard to pray divinely. On which day he said to the doctor, 'I thought to have been dissolved [dead] ere now.'

The pastor answered, 'My Lord, weary not of the Lord's yoke. Jesus Christ is posting [travelling] fast to be at you: he is within few miles.'

He answered mildly, 'This is my infirmity. I will wait on [continue waiting]; he is worthy the on-waiting. Though he be long in coming, yet I dare say he is coming, leaping over the mountains and skipping over the hills. If he were once come, we should not sunder [separate].'

The pastor answered, 'Some have gotten in this same life their full [fill] of Christ, howbeit Christ is oft under a mask to his own in this life and will have them kissing him through a mask, yet even his best saints—Job, David, Jeremiah—were under desertions.'

My Lord answered, 'What are their examples to me? I am not in holiness near to Job, David, or Jeremiah.'

The pastor answered, 'It is true my Lord, you cannot take such wide steps as they did, but you are in the same way with them. A young child followeth his father at the back [behind him]. Though he cannot take such wide steps as he, yet this hindereth him not to be in the same way with him. My Lord, your hunger overcometh your faith. Only but believe his word. You are longing for Christ; only believe Jesus Christ is faithful and will come quickly.'

To this my Lord answered, 'I think it time. Lord Jesus, come!'

Then the pastor said, 'My Lord, our nature is in trouble [is at pains] to be wholly upon our own deliverance, whereas God seeketh first to be glorified in our faith and patience and hope, and then it is time enough that we be delivered.

He answered, 'Good reason, my Lord be first served. Lord give me to wait on. Only, Lord, burn me not to dross.'

Another said, 'Cast back your eyes, my Lord, upon that which you have received and be thankful.' At the hearing whereof he presently broke forth in praising of God, and finding himself weak, and his speech failing, some more than an hour before death, he desired the pastor to pray, which he did.

After prayer the pastor cried in his ear, 'My Lord, may you now sunder [part] with Christ.' He said nothing, nor was it expected he should speak any more. Yet a little after, the pastor asked, 'Have you any sense of the Lord's love?' He answered, 'I have sense.'

The pastor said, 'Do you not enjoy?' He answered, 'I do enjoy.'

Thereafter the pastor said, 'Will ye not sunder [part] with Christ?' He answered, 'By no means.' This was the last word, not being able to speak any more.

The pastor asked if he should pray. He turned his eye towards the pastor. In the time of that last prayer he was observed joyfully smiling and looking up with glorious looks, as was observed by the beholders, and with a certain beauty. His visage was beautified, as beautiful as ever he was in his life. He expired with loud and strong fetches [cries] and sobs, being strong of heart and body, of the age of five and thirty years. The expiring of his breath, the ceasing of the motion of his pulse (which the physician was still gripping) trysted [coincided] all precisely with the 'Amen' of his prayer.

And so died he sweetly and holily, and his end was peace. He departed about the setting of the sun, September 12, 1634.

Blessed are they who die in the Lord

ℰℛ

Made in the USA
Columbia, SC
02 December 2021

50263490R00043